A HORSE NAMED PARIS

A Horse Named Paris

BY LYNN SONBERG

PHOTOGRAPHS BY

KEN ROBBINS

BRADBURY PRESS
New York

Text copyright © 1986 by Lynn Sonberg
Photographs copyright © 1986 by Ken Robbins
Bradbury Press
An Affiliate of Macmillan, Inc.
866 Third Avenue, New York, NY 10022
Collier Macmillan Canada, Inc.
Printed and bound in Japan

10 9 8 7 6 5 4 3 2 1

The text of this book is set in 14 pt. Galliard.
The illustrations are black-and-white photographs which were
hand-tinted by the photographer and printed in full-color.
Book design by Kathleen Westray and Ed Sturmer,
Design and Printing Productions, New York

Library of Congress Cataloging-in-Publication Data
Sonberg, Lynn.   A horse named Paris.
Summary: Text and photographs depict how eleven-year-old Amanda
Kraus cares for, rides, and enjoys her horse Paris.
1. Horses— Juvenile literature. 2. Horsemanship—
Juvenile literature. [1. Horses. 2. Horsemanship.
3. Kraus, Amanda]   I. Robbins, Ken, ill.   II. Title.
SF302.S664 1986 636.1 86-6886
ISBN 0-02-786260-7

FOR NORMA JEAN,
who also saw the magic
L. S.

FOR KATE O'BRIEN
K. R.

ACKNOWLEDGMENTS

Our thanks to Amanda Kraus and Maggie Kotuk for generously sharing their time and their special world, and for their unfailing good humor, good horsemanship, and good company. We are also indebted to Steve Latham, and to Charles Teetor for his gracious permission to photograph Westernese Farm.

INTRODUCTION

SOME horses live on farms. Others live on large ranches. Still others are kept by families on their own land. A few roam free in the wild.

Many people love horses but don't have time to care for them or enough land for grazing. If they want a horse, they must board it at a stable. All horses need a clean stall, the right food, and a pasture or paddock. A boarding fee covers these basic necessities and varies from stable to stable.

This book is about Paris, a dapple gray horse who is boarded at a small stable called Westernese Farm on Long Island, New York. Ten other horses and a pony named Cutie live there, too.

P A R I S is a pleasure horse. In the past he competed at horse shows but now he is ridden by his owner, Amanda Kraus, just for fun.

WHEN the weather is warm and fair, the horses at Westernese farm run free in the pasture all day and all night. Early in the morning, and just before sunset the horses are given hay and grain. The grain is placed in buckets, which are hung along the fence.

Paris is given vitamins, four quarts of sweet feed, and four alfalfa cubes at each meal.

In the winter, or when the weather is bad, the horses eat and spend the night in their stalls. In the morning, they are let out to pasture.

When Paris first came to the stable, he tried to boss the other horses. He would chase a new horse away, and nip or kick a horse that tried to lead the herd. Sometimes there were fights.

Recently, a young black horse named Nonny came to the stable. Paris and Nonny usually stay near each other in the pasture. Nonny doesn't seem to mind being bossed and Paris has been calmer since he arrived.

EVERY six weeks, the farrier visits the stable to shoe the horses. A horse doesn't need shoes when it is let out to pasture but if it is ridden on hard roads or jumped over fences, its hooves need to be protected.

Paris's old shoes are removed, and his hooves are trimmed with a sharp knife until they are level and smooth. A horse's hooves are like a person's nails. They keep growing and must be shortened. The farrier then heats the new shoes in a forge until they are hot. Then he hammers them into the shape of the horse's hooves.

None of this hurts Paris, since horses have no feeling in their hooves. The farrier though, is sometimes kicked by a nervous horse—but never by Paris.

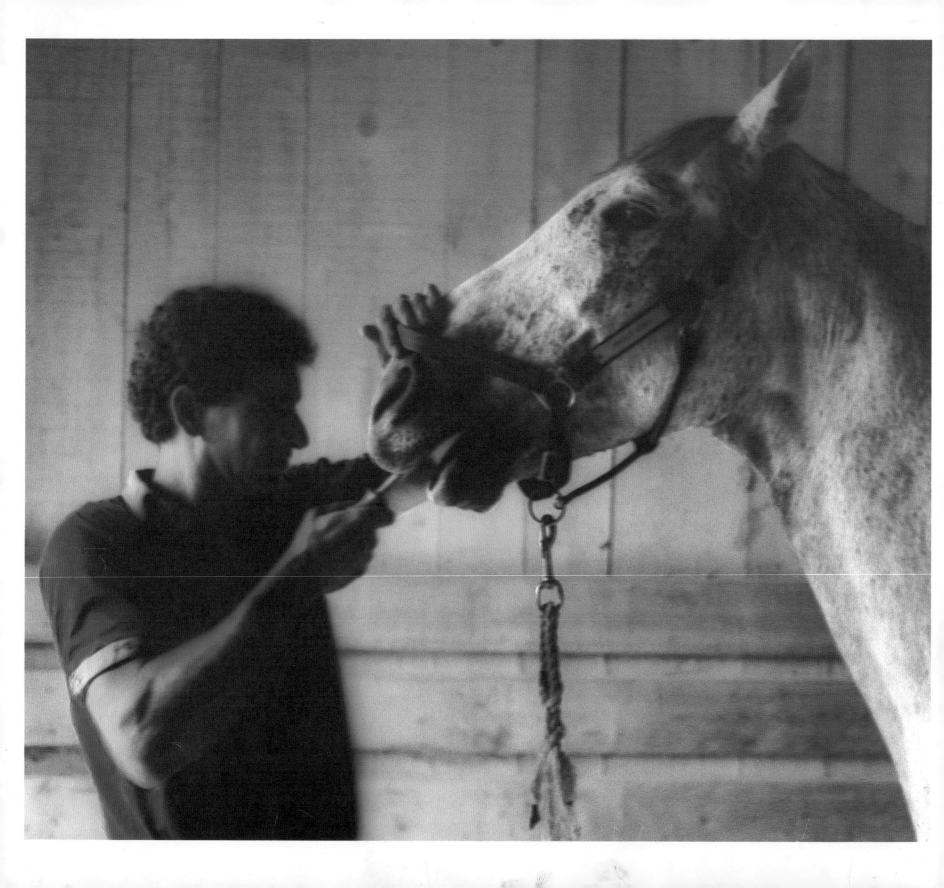

PARIS has never been sick, but one summer he cut his nostril on the latch to his stall, and the veterinarian stitched it. The wound had to be soaked every day. Amanda put sliced apples in a bucket of fresh water and when Paris dunked for the apples, the cut was cleaned.

Every six months the veterinarian worms Paris and sometimes gives him shots. Paris's teeth need regular care too. Unless they are filed twice a year, the edges become sharp and jagged which prevents him from chewing properly.

Paris sometimes backs away from the file when the vet tries to put it in his mouth. But when the vet speaks sharply to him, Paris stands still.

To KEEP Paris looking tidy, his mane and forelock are shortened a few times each year. Amanda wraps his hair around a special comb and pulls out the longer hairs. Horses have few nerve endings at the roots of their hair so pulling it out doesn't hurt.

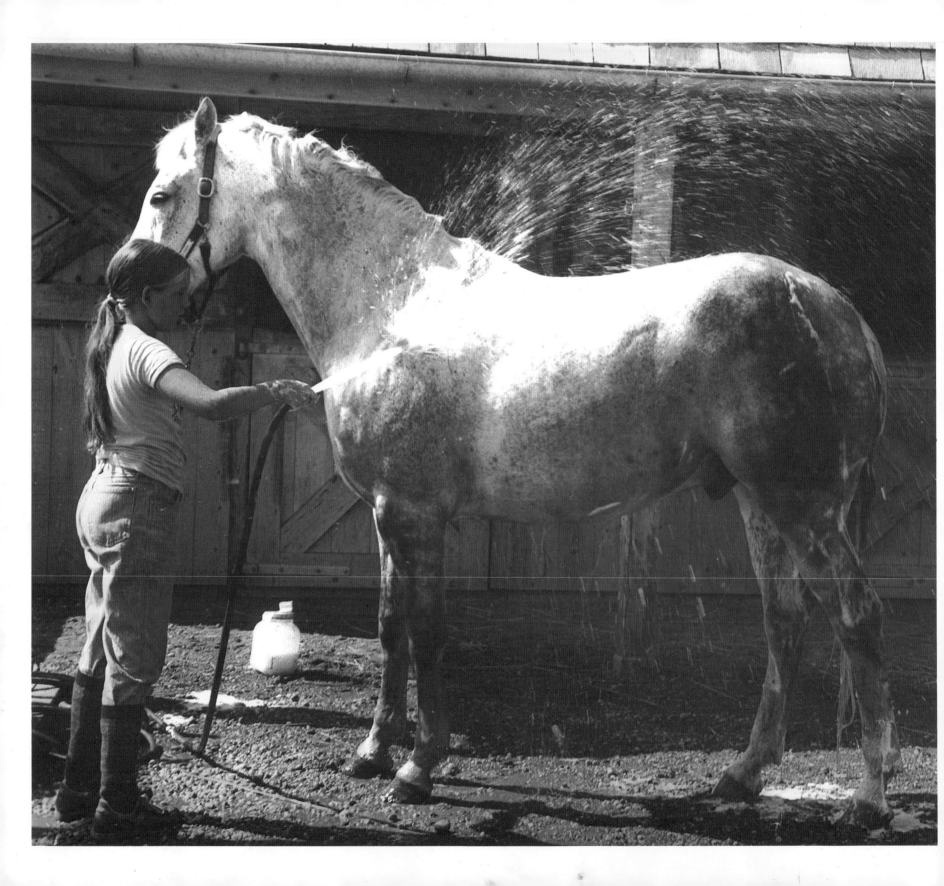

PARIS'S light gray coat shows every bit of dirt. When the weather is warm, he is hosed and bathed. Special horse shampoo is used to make his coat shine.

Amanda is very careful not to spray water in his ears. A little water can lead to infection or if water blocks the ear, a horse can lose its balance.

MUCKING out Paris's stall isn't fun, but it should be done every day. A dirty stall will attract flies and may also cause thrush, a serious hoof disease.

Paris, like all horses, needs daily exercise to maintain good muscle tone. He gets some exercise when he is at pasture but that is not enough to prepare him for jumping or hard trail rides.

Sometimes Amanda exercises Paris on a lunge line, a long rope attached to Paris's halter. While holding the rope, Amanda tells Paris to move in a large circle around her. If he doesn't move at the right pace, she urges him forward by cracking a long whip.

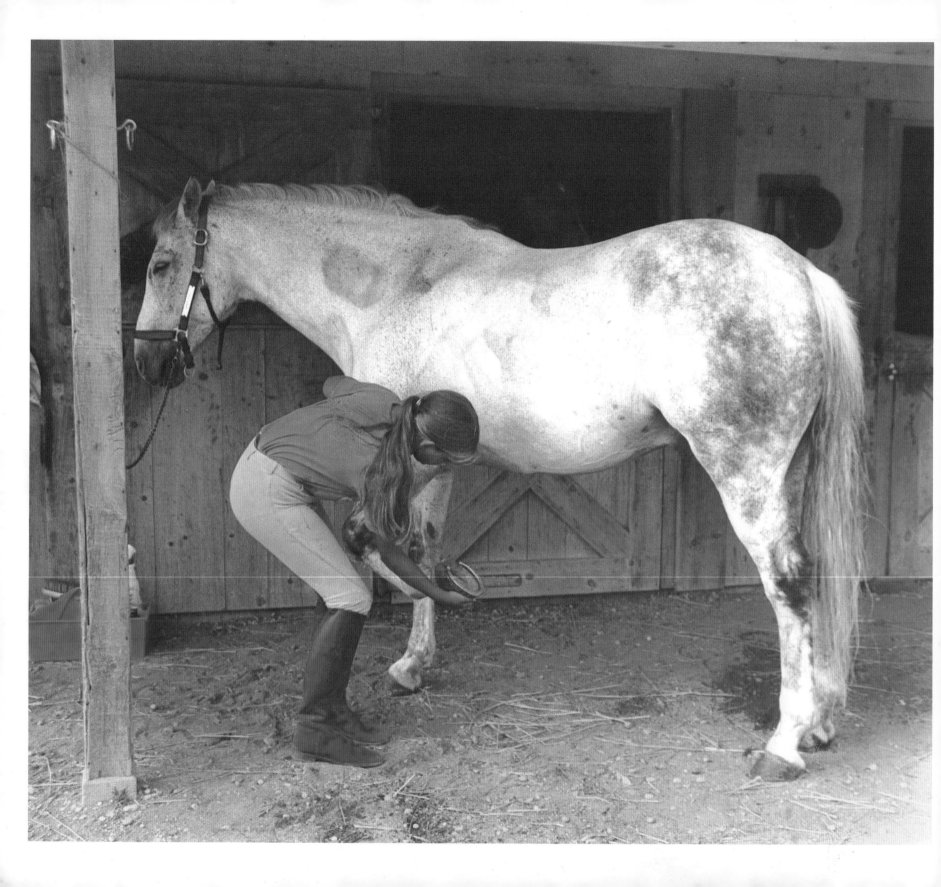

IT CAN take half an hour or more to get Paris ready to ride. First he is brought in from the pasture and groomed with a currycomb and dandy brush. Loose hair and dirt come to the surface and are brushed away. His eyes and nose are cleaned with a sponge. Then his coat is rubbed with a soft cloth to make it shine. His hooves are cleaned with a metal pick and a dressing is applied to keep them from drying out.

Grooming helps Paris look his best; it also prevents injuries. Riding Paris over a hard surface with a stone in his hoof, could cause him to go lame, and dirt under his saddle could cause a sore.

PARIS'S saddle and bridle are kept in the tack room. When the door is left open, Amanda often finds Cutie in there, nosing around. The tack room is cool, and Cutie sometimes finds apple cores in the trash basket.

It would be easy to keep Cutie in her stall, or in her paddock, but she is more fun than trouble to have around.

EVEN though Paris is tall, it isn't hard for Amanda to put on his bridle. He lowers his head to make it easier. Getting his saddle on right is trickier. Sometimes Paris puffs up his belly when Amanda tries to tighten the leather strap, or girth, that holds the saddle on his back. When this happens, Amanda waits until Paris lets out his breath, then she tightens the girth again.

Amanda wears a hard hat and boots when she rides. Should she fall, the hat will protect her head and the heels on her boots will prevent her feet from sliding through the stirrups.

A HORSE and rider are partners. Neither one can look good or perform well unless the other is doing exactly the right thing.

Like most well-trained horses, Paris knows how to jump over fences and move correctly when he's ridden at a walk, a trot, or a canter. A canter is a smooth, slow gallop; it feels a little like sitting in a rocking chair.

A GOOD horse can enable a rider to perform at his or her best, but the rider must always tell the horse what to do. When Amanda wants Paris to trot, she presses both legs against his sides. If she wants him to canter to the right, she shortens her reins, sits deep in the saddle, and squeezes her left leg against his side. When she wants to stop, she sits back and pulls gently on the reins. Legs, hands, and body position must always work smoothly together.

Paris is much stronger than Amanda, so Amanda cannot force him to do what she wants. He must be alert and obey her commands. Most of the time, Paris is a willing partner. But sometimes he is cranky and stubborn. Amanda must then work even harder to make him "listen."

PARIS is difficult to control when he jumps. His previous owner trained him as a speed jumper, and he often jumps at a breakneck pace. Sometimes he does not obey Amanda. Once he ran away with her at a horse show.

Trotting over rails on the ground is a good warm-up before jumping. The rails, called *cavalletti,* are placed a stride apart. To avoid stepping on the rails, Paris has to lift his legs which forces him to pay attention to his footing.

ONCE in a while, the people at the stable organize a special event on the cross-country course. This course is a series of jumps that are similar to the natural obstacles found on a hunt course. There are fifteen jumps in open fields and in the woods.

Each person rides at a canter over the mile-long course. Points are taken off if a horse refuses to go over any of the jumps.

Paris is the best jumper at the stable.

PARIS and the other horses are sometimes taken on trail rides. There are still many miles of wooded trails, open meadows, and wildlife preserves near the stable.

Local farmers allow riders along the edge of their fields, as long as they do not trample the crops.

IN MIDSUMMER Amanda likes to canter between rows of tall sweet corn. She always rides with her heels lower than her toes, which will prevent her from falling in case Paris shies.

Horses are easily frightened by sudden or unfamiliar sights and sounds. Even though Paris is not a nervous horse, something can happen on a trail ride to make him shy, or jump sideways: a rabbit or deer may leap across the trail, or a startled bird may fly out of the bushes.

HORSES are less likely to shy at the ocean beach where there are few places for animals and birds to hide. Beach rides are best on a calm day so the horses won't get excited by the wind and the roar of the surf.

Amanda always rides Paris on the hard-packed sand near the water's edge. Cantering or trotting on soft deep sand can strain a horse's legs.

IN THE summer the horses are ridden to the bay to go swimming. This is fun for the riders, and the cool water is good for the horses' legs.

Some horses cannot be coaxed into the water, but Paris is perfectly willing to go swimming. Amanda takes off his saddle so it won't be ruined by the salt water.

When a ride is over, Paris's saddle and bridle are removed. If his chest feels hot, he is walked around the paddock until he cools down. Then his coat is brushed to get rid of the sweat marks.

SOMETIMES Paris rolls on the ground after a ride.

IN THE evening, Amanda often visits Paris to say good-night.
Paris is Amanda's special friend.